YOU SAID A MOUTHFUL

Roger Karshner

Dramaline Publications
10470 Riverside, Drive, Suite #201
Toluca Lake, CA 91602
818/985-9148
Fax: 818/985-0408

Cover Art: Rod Dyer Group

This book is printed on 55# Glatfelter acid-free paper. A paper that meets the requirements of the American Standard of Permanence of paper for printed library material.

INTRODUCTION

I'm sure everyone has heard the expression, "That's easy for you to say." Well, for many of us normal folks sometimes things aren't all that easy to spit out—our tongues get in the way of our eye teeth and we can't see what we're saying. Certain combinations and arrangements of words are difficult to untangle and they come out sounding like "Zymtvpt." Or they scramble themselves in our mouths resulting in stupid and often embarrassing outpourings. Heck, we've all done it one time or another. And overcoming this problem and learning to mouth meaty morsels mellifluously is a real challenge for our tongues.

Way back around 350 B.C. legend has it that Demosthenes, the great Athenian orator and statesman, honed his diction by speaking with stones in his mouth. And Richard Burton stood by the seashore shouting Shakespeare to the pounding surf as a means of improving his delivery. While these methods may be cogent to the development of clean speech they are also generally impractical if not downright ludicrous. Running around with a face full of rocks would not only be an uncomfortable experience, it would also most certainly attract looks of utmost derision. And what if you swallowed one of those suckers? And screaming the Bard at the surf is indeed difficult if you live in, say, Flagstaff, Arizona. What then is the practical and most effective alternative? Why tongue twisters, of course.

Tongue twisters date back hundreds of years and their sources are wide and varied. Peter Piper and his famous Peppers were being twisted in the seventeenth century. And one suspects that the origin of twisters goes way back of this. Back to the cave dwellers perhaps—who knows? But we do know that tongue twisters have been around a long time and that they are a great source of amusement and fun and that they are wonderful antidotes for lazy speech, particularly wonderful for actors and singers, and public speakers who rely on the spoken word as a means of making a buck.

There are thousands of tongue twisters and they come from all over. The ones in this book were selected because I felt they were most representative of the best and would most effectively improve lip flexibility, help with the "s" and "r' sounds, alleviate the lazy palate, address the problem of the closely placed "sh" and "s," and would definitely improve your speech.

Remember: Always practice twisters aloud, and attempt to spit them out as fast as possible, and with the utmost clarity. The short lines—like "Shining soldiers"—should be repeated rapidly, cleanly *five* times. Be bold—go for it!

So go at it. Get those pretzels out of your tongue. Improve your speech, amaze your friends, and . . . have fun!

RK

Betty bit a bit of butter,
But it was a bitter bite;
But a bit of better butter
Betty never bit.

Suddenly swerving, seven small swans
Swam silently southward,
Seeing six swift sailboats
Sailing sedately seaward.

Peggy Babcock.

Big Bill Billiken blew bursting bubbles
by billions.

Tongue twisters twist tongues twisted
Trying to untangle twisted tangles:
My tang's tungled now.

The twister of twists,
Once twisted a twist,
And the twist that he twisted,
Was a three-twisted twist.
Now in twisting this twist,
If a twist should untwist,
The twist that untwisted
Would untwist the twist.

Did you ever see a 'possum
In a one-pole pig-pen
Picking up papaws
Putting in his pockets?

Red roses rustle rurally.

A sick sparrow sang six sad spring songs
sitting sheltering under a squat shrub.

The city sweep shook his sooty sheet in the city street.

1

Pink silk socks with shot silk spots.

If Roland Reynolds rolled a round roll
Round and round a room, where is the round roll which
Roland Reynolds rolled round the room?

Here's to it and to it again,
If you ever get to it do do it
And don't do it,
Here's hoping you'll never get to it
To do it again.

How much caramel can a canny cannibal
cram into a camel, if a canny cannibal can
cram caramel into a camel?

Freddy thrush flies through thick fog.

Lloyd George.

Hath Hazel asthma?

Should such a shapeless sash such shabby
stitches show?

Shining soldiers.

A box of biscuits,
A box of mixed biscuits,
And a biscuit mixer.

Thelma saw thistles in the thick thatch.

Can Kitty cuddle Clara's kitten?

James just jostled Jean.

Jock sopped flop-sweat

Brisk brave brigadiers brandished broad bright
blades, blunderbusses, and bludgeons.

Which switch is the switch, Miss, for Ipswich?
It's the Ipswich switch which I require.
Which switch is the switch, Miss, for Ipswich?
You switched me on the wrong wire.
You switched me on Norwich, not Ipswich,
So now to prevent further hitch,
If you'll tell me, Miss, which switch is Norwich
And which switch is Ipswich,
I'll know which to switch.

Six skyscrapers stood snugly side by side
shimmering by the seashore.

Soldiers shudder when shrill shells shriek.

A tutor who tooted a flute
Tried to tutor two tooters to toot.
Said the two to the tutor,
"Is it harder to toot or
To tutor two tooters to toot?"

The gum glue grew glum.

Ned Nott was shot and Sam Shott was not.
So it's better to be Shott than Nott.
Some say Nott was not shot, but Shott swears
he shot Nott.
Either the shot Shott shot at Nott was not shot
or Nott was not shot.
If the shot Shott shot shot Nott, Nott was shot,
But if the shot Shott shot shot Shott himself, then
Shott would be shot and Nott would not.
However, the shot Shott shot shot not Shott but
Nott.
It's not easy to say who was shot and who was not,
But we know who was Shott and who was Nott.

We eat what we can, and what we can't
we can.

The short sort shoot straight through.

Coop up the cook!

One smart feller he felt smart;
Two smart fellers they both felt smart;
Three smart fellers they all felt smart.

A maid with a duster
Made a furious bluster
Dusting a bust in the hall.
When the bust was dusted,
The bust it was busted,
The bust it was dust, that is all.

Susan shineth shoes and socks,
Socks and shoes shineth Susan.
She ceaseth shining shoes and socks,
For socks and shoes shock Susan.

A hundred air-inhaling elephants.

The bottom of the butter bucket is the
buttered bucket bottom.

Esaw Wood sawed wood. Esaw Wood would
saw wood. Oh, the wood that Wood would saw!
One day Esaw Wood saw a saw saw wood as no
other woodsaw Wood ever saw would saw wood.
Of all the woodsaws Wood ever saw saw wood,
Wood never saw a woodsaw that would saw like
the wood-saw Wood saw would. Now Esaw saws with
that saw he saw saw wood.

Sunshine Susie shone her shoes with soap and shoe
shine.

Jock Jones jumped jerkily on Jimmy at the juvenile
sports last June.

Peter Prangle,
The prickly prangly pear picker,
Picked three pecks
Of prangly pears from
The prickly prangly pear trees
On the pleasant prairies.

The broom blooms when the bluebells bloom.

Rupert wrestled rashly with Robin.

A fly flew past Flo's flat,
And a fly flew past fat Flo.
Is the fly that flew past Flo
This same fly that flew past fat Flo's flat?

How many cans can a canner can
If a canner can can cans?
A canner can can as many cans
As a canner can if a canner can can cans.

Petty Kitty Creighton had a cotton batten cat.
The cotton batten cat was bitten by a rat.
The kitten that was bitten had a button for an eye,
And bitting off the button made the cotton
batten fly.

cute

Of all the felt I ever felt,
I never felt a piece a felt,
That felt the same as that felt felt,
When first I felt the felt of that felt hat.

good

Fish and chip shop chips are soft chips.

Figs form fine fancy fare.

I do like cheap sea trips,
Cheap sea trips on ships.
I like to be on the deep blue sea,
When the ship rolls and dips.

Six sixpences stood shimmering on a shop counter.

If a doctor doctored another doctor,
Would the doctor doing the doctoring
Doctor the other doctor
In the way the doctored doctor wanted to be
doctored,
Or would the doctor doing the doctoring
Doctor the other doctor
In his own way?

Billy Burton buttoned his bright brown boots
and blue coat before breakfast began.

An oyster met an oyster,
And they were oysters two;
Two oysters met two oysters,
And they were oysters too;
Four oysters met a pint of milk,
And they were oyster stew.

Any noise annoys an oyster, but a noisy noise annoys an
oyster most.

Shave a cedar shingle thin.

There was once a bonnie Scotch laddie
Who said, as he took off his plaiddie,
"I've just had a dish
Of awful good fish,"
What had he had, had he had haddie?

The strapping soldiers strived sternly to strengthen the
stronghold.

The Duke paid the money due to the Jew before
the dew was off the grass on Tuesday, and the Jew
having duly acknowledged it said adieu to the Duke
forever.

Sidney Shelly thrust six thick sticks through
sixty-six ricks.

Dashing Daniel defied David to deliver Dora
from the dawning danger.

Who washed Washington's white woolen
underwear when Washington's washerwoman
went West?

The suitor wore shorts and a short shooting suit
to a short shoot. But the shorts didn't suit the short
shooting suit and at the short shoot the short shooting
suit didn't suit. Oh shoot!

Christopher Twistle was trying to whistle and
Christopher twisted his tongue.

The mighty master murdered the maddened
magistrate.

A regal rural ruler.

Suddenly swerving, seven small swans
Swam silently southward,
Seeing six swift sailboats
Sailing sedately seaward.

Weak writers want white ruled writing paper.

Gertrude Gray gazed at the grey goose gaily.

Six southern sailors sailing southern seas.

Which witch had the wen on her hand when we met
them and you asked them whether we should have fine
weather?

Angels oiled the hinges on her oil engine with
oil-engine oil.

Old, oily Ollie oils oily autos.

Sally Sloop saw six sad sheep standing on the sea shore
shamelessly shamming sleep.

The old school scold sold
The school coal scuttle:
If the old school scold sold
The school coal scuttle,
The school should scold
And scuttle the old school scold.

He ate hot apples and halibut hastily.

Flora's fan fluttered feebly and her fine fingers fidgeted.

Sammy sitting singing
Sought Susie Shaw,
So Susie started sobbing,
So Sammy stopped searching.

Amidst the mists and coldest frosts
With barest wrists and stoutest boasts
He thrusts his fists against the posts
But still insists he sees the ghosts.

The cows graze gracefully in Farmer Thicklewaite's
thicket.

"Goodbye, Gertie," gushed Gussie.
"Goodbye Gussie," gushed Gertie.

If thee and thy folks
Liked me and my folks
Like me and my folks
Like thee and thy folks,
They'd come and see a body.
There never were folks liked folks
Since folks were folks
Like me and my folks
Like thee and thy folks.

Stella stole stealthily to the strand.

Nine naughty nanny goats nibbled nine nice new
nasturtiums.

Seventeen slimy slugs in satin sunbonnets sat singing
short sad songs.

You sent me your bill, Berry,
Before it was due, Berry;
Your father, the elder Berry,
Had not been such a goose, Berry.

Peter Palmer painted a paper peacock, purple, pink,
and puce.

Big blue blisters bleeding badly.

I can't stand rotten writin' when it's written rotten.

A flea and a fly in a flue
Were imprisoned. Oh, what could they do?
Said the flea, "Let us fly!"
Said the fly, "Let us flee!"
So they flew through a flaw in the flue.

Maggie McGregor makes magnificent macaroons.

Can you imagine an imaginary menagerie manager
imagining managing an imaginary menagerie?

A white witch watched a woebegone walrus winding
white wool.

Betty beat a bit of better butter to make a better batter.

Mister Matthew Mathers, my math master, munches
mashed marmalade muffins.

Fritz Fischer fishes for fresh fish.
Fresh fish fish for Fritz Fischer.

"Go, my son, and shut the shutter,"
This I heard a mother utter.
"Shutter's shut," the boy did mutter,
"I can't shut 'er any shutter."

Rascally ruffians robbed the regent.

I was barbarously barbarized
By the barbarity of a barbarian barber
In the barber's barbarizing shop.

Diderot dined on the back of a plump turkey.

The owner of the Inside Inn
Was outside his Inside Inn,
With his inside outside his Inside Inn.

The hedge hindered the homicide from hurting himself.

If a hair net could net hair,
How much hair could that hair net net,
If a hair net could net hair?

Six cents for these sausages?

In Huron, a hewer, Hugh Hughes,
Hewed yews of unusual hues.
Hugh Hughes used blue yews
To build sheds for his ewes;
So his ewes a blue-hued ewe-shed use.

His beard descending swept his aged breast.

When does the wrist watch strap shop shut?

Ships lie shattered on the shingle.

The green grub goes to the green grass.

A rhinoceros rushed into a restaurant and ordered ribs of beef, rabbit, rolls, raspberries, radishes, rhubarb pie, and rice.

If a Hottentot taught a Hottentot tot
To talk ere the tot could not totter,
Ought the Hottentot tot
Be taught to say aught, or naught,
Or what ought to be taught her?
If to hoot and to toot a Hottentot to
Be taught by her Hottentot tutor,
Ought the tutor get hot
If the Hottentot tot
Hoot and toot at her Hottentot tot?

Shears have sharp shining points.

She says she shall sew a sheet.

Sixty-six shy school masters sailing serenely a ship on a shining sea.

Dimpled Dinah danced in dainty dimity down the dunes.

The minx mixed a medicinal mixture.

11

I wish I hadn't washed this wrist watch.
I've washed all the wheels and works,
Oh how it jumps and jerks.
I wish I hadn't washed this watch,
For I would wish a washer woman where
I wished this wrist watch which was washed.

If a dog chews shoes what shoes should he choose to chew?

Paul, an inexperienced painter, painted pills cheaply.

A yellow yo-yo young Hubert used.

The masts mask the majestic mansions and the multitudinous minarets.

A plain pinewood police van,
Privately packed with protesting passengers,
Plies periodically to Plymouth prison.

Valiant vassals vexed Victoria.

Say, did you say, or did you not say
What I said you said?
For it is said that you said
That you did not say
What I said you said.
Now if you say that you did not say
What I said you said,
Then what do you say you did say instead
Of what I said you said?

Vera vaulted the valley violets.

Four famous fishermen found four flounders (flippers flapping furiously) faithfully following four floppy female fatfish.

Five frantic fat frogs fled from fifty fierce fishes.

Three sad tigers threshing wheat in a wheat field.

You've no need to light a night light
On a light night like tonight,
For a night light's light's a slight light,
And tonight's a night that's light.
When a night's light, like tonight's light,
It is really not quite right
To light night lights with their slight lights
On a light night like tonight.

A crow flew over the river with a lump of raw liver.

What's here was there.
There's what was here.

Whistle for the thistle sifter.

A thin little boy picked six thick thistle sticks.

Buy only a little brown cape, for he who buys only a
little brown cape pays only for a little brown cape.

A batch of biscuits,
A box of biscuits,
A batch of mixed biscuits,
A box of mixed biscuits,
A basket of mixed biscuits
And a brief beef brisket.

I shot three thrushes.
You shoot three shy thrushes.

The coon crooned crazily in the corn.

Quinn's twin sisters sing tongue twisters.

If the hobo's nose is the color of the rose
And the hobo's hose have holes in the toes
And the hobo hoes where the tater grows,
How do you suppose
Anyone knows
How many rows
The hobo hoes?

Mrs. Cripp's cat crept into the crypt, crept around, and crept out through a crack.

The squirrel squeals with breathalysing indignation, quiveringly spluttering complete repudiation of the impossibly preposterous allegation of gross intoxication.

I was looking back to see
If she was looking back to see
If I was looking back to see
If she was looking back at me.

Granny's grey goose greedily gobbled golden grain in Graham's gabled granary.

As the roaring rocket rose,
The restless roosters rollicked.

Gladys glanced gaily at Grace and glided glitteringly past Greta at the Gala.

A poor pauper paused on purpose to pawn a porpoise.

The lone lovers left the leafy lane.

Crows graze in droves on grass which grows on graves in groves.

The trend of the times was tiresome, tedious and tame.

A noisy noise annoys an oyster.

She sells seashells on the sea shore.
The shells she sells are seashells, I'm sure.
So if she sells seashells on the seashore,
I'm sure she sells seashore shells.

All I want is a proper cup of coffee,
Made in a proper coffee pot.
You can believe it or not . . .
I want a cup of coffee
In a proper coffee pot.
Tin coffee pots or iron coffee pots,
They're no use to me.
If I can't have a
Proper cup of coffee
In a proper copper coffee pot,
I'll have a cup of tea.

Swim, Sam, swim;
Show them you're some swimmer.
Six sharp sharks are out to take your liver—
So swim, Sam, swim.

When a twister a-twisting will twist him a twist,
For the twining his twist he three twines doth entwist;
But if one of the twines of the twist do untwist,
The twine that untwisteth, untwisteth the twist.
Untwirling the twine that untwisteth between,
He twists with his twister the twain in a twine;
Then twice having twisted the twines of the twine,
He twisteth the twines he had twisted in vain.
The twain that, in twisting before in the twine,
As twines are entwisted, he now doth untwine,
'Twixt the twain intertwisting a twine more between,
He, twisting his twister, makes a twist of the twine.

The strenuous struggle seemed superfluous.

Cows graze in groves on grass which grows in grooves
in groves.

15

The Pope poked a poker at the piper.
So the piper poked some pepper at the Pope.

Two toads totally tried trying to trot to Tidsbury.

The big black-backed bumblebee.

There was a young man named Fischer
Who fished for a fish in a fissure.
The fish with a grin
Pulled the fisherman in;
Now they're fishing the fissure for Fischer.

The suitability of a suet pudding without superfluous
plums is a superstition presumably due to Susan's true
economy.

Timothy took Titus to Tavistock to teach the tomtits to
talk theology to the Turks that travel through Tartary.

The tracker tracked and tricked and trapped the tricky
trickster.

"S" on a wall stands for Spacious Sewers where saucy
sewermen sometimes spend Saturdays and Sundays,
scouring scented slime for slothful slugs and setting
subtle snares for sleepy snails.

A critical cricket critic.

I would if I could
If I couldn't, how could I?
I couldn't, without I could, could I?
Could you, without you could, could you?
Could you, could you?
Could you, without you could, could you?

Swedish swordswallowers shift short swords swiftly.

Sister Susie's sewing shirts for soldiers.
Some skill at sewing shirts our shy young Susie shows.
Some soldiers sent epistles,
Say they'd sooner sleep on thistles
Than the saucy soft short shirts for soldiers
Sister Susie sews.

Old Dunn,
Young Dunn,
And Old Dunn's son.
Young Dunn,
Will be Dunn,
When Old Dunn's done.

Four fat dogs frying fritters and fiddling ferociously.

Whether the weather be fine, or whether the weather
    be not,
Whether the weather be cold, of the weather be hot,
We'll weather the weather, whatever the weather,
Whether we like it or not.

George Grabs grabs crabs,
Crabs George Grabs grabs.
If George Grabs grabs crabs,
Where are the crabs George grabs?

Gloria Groot glued a groat to Gregory's goat.

A coster carried cabbages across a crooked court.

The truants tramp trustingly towards Troon.

Five French friars fanning a fainted flea.

Will you, won't you,
Do you, don't you,
Aren't you goin' to,
Can't I coax you—Ah, please!

Tommy Tye
Tried to tie his tie,
But tugging too tight
Tore his tie.
He turned to Ted,
Told Ted to try
To tie the tie
Tom tried to tie.

This lute, with its flute-like tones, was captured in the loot of a great city, and its luminous sides are made of unpolluted silver.

Tiny Tim toddles to the tiny toddlers' toyshop.

Six steaming sheiks, sitting stitching sheets.

Something whistled past his head.
"A miss again!" his Missus said.

Six slippery seals slinking silently ashore.

There was a young lady named Sue
Who'd a date to dine at 8:02—
She got there at 8
Too hungry to wait
So her tete-a-tete ate at 8 too.

Ziggy zigged whapping Zacks back with a look of crunching snarls.

Lambert the liver lover loved liver but liver made Mrs. Lambert quiver so Lambert ate alone because liver made his missus' liver shiver.

Stanley sat sadly solitary sipping sodas sloppily near the Mississippi.

Rick's spitz Fritz threw snits and fits.

Sammy Simpson smiled slowly.
"Surely Sylvia swims!" said Sammy, surprised.
"Somebody should show Sylvia some strokes so she shan't sink."
Sylvia seemed serious, so Sammy swam six strong strokes.
"So simple," said Sammy.
Soon Sylvia started swimming.
"Splendid!" shouted Sammy.
"She swims spiffingly."
Sylvia seemed somewhat surprised.
She swam several strokes—splashed—sank!
"Save Sylvia!" screamed Sammy,
Swimming swiftly shorewards.
Seizing Sylvia, Sammy shouted shrilly.
Some ships soon saw Sammy's serious situation.
Six stalwart sailors saved Sylvia.
"Silly Sylvia," sighed Sammy, shivering slightly.
"She shouldn't start swimming so suddenly."
Sylvia swallowed swiftly.
"Stupid!" she shouted sharply.
Sammy seemed shocked.
"Sorry, Sylvia," said Sammy.
So Sylvia smiled sweetly.

Roads close, so snow slows shows.

Six silent snakes slithering slowly southward.

The seething sea ceaseth
And thus—The seething sea sufficeth us.

There was a young lady named Kate
Who went out to dine at 8:08,
It would be hard to relate
At this very late date
What Kate and her tete-a-tete ate at 8:08.

Lesser leather never weathered lesser wetter weather.

Lotty loves lollies when lolling in the lobby.

High roller,
Low roller,
Lower a roller.

A rat ran leaping round.
Run rat, leap rat.
Or the cat will catch you.

Six selfish shellfish.

A stewed sow's snout, a sow's snout stewed.

The swan swims—
The swan swam—
The swimming swan swam to the sea.

Plain plump Pansy played piquet pleasantly.

Merry merry moments makes Madge mischievous.

Eight gay geese grazing gaily into Greece.

Twenty talented teachers teaching tiny tots their twice
times table.

Good better best,
Never let it rest,
Till your good is better,
And your better best.

Buster Bailey fasted at the Astor.

Would you pawn prawns at a pawn shop or
prawn shop?

The swiftly swirling mill wheel grinds the
gleaming grain.

Mr. Inside went over to see Mr. Outside. Mr. Inside
stood outside and called to Mr. Outside inside. Mr.
Outside answered Mr. Inside from inside and told Mr.
Inside to come inside. Mr. Inside said, "No," for Mr.
Outside to come inside. Mr. Outside and Mr. Inside
argued from inside and outside about going outside or
coming inside. Finally, Mr. Inside coaxed Mr. Outside
to come outside, instead of Mr. Outside having Mr.
Inside come inside, and both Mr. Outside and Mr. Inside
went to the riverside and committed suicide.

Who washed
Washington's white woolen underwear
When Washington's washerwoman went west?
Washington's wife wouldn't wash
Washington's white woolen underwear
When Washington's washerwoman went west,
So—
George Washington unwillingly washed
Washington's white woolen underwear
When Washington's washerwoman went west.

Many mincing maidens meandered moodily moorwards.

Is there any pleasant peasant present?

Bluebeard brought back black bric-a-brac.

Battling Bill bullied the blustering brigand beside the
bunker.

Last year I could not hear with either ear.

Sixty-six sickly chicks.

Cut Clara's cauliflower and catch crawling crabs,
Caroline.

The courtiers could not curb the cruel Calvinist.

A tar bought two tarts from a Tartar.
Said the tar to the Tartar, "Too tart are these tarts. Now,
a tart made of cream o' tart—"
But, "Ta-ta!" to the tar said the Tartar.

If a chicken and a half
Laid an egg and a half
In a day and a half,
The farmer wouldn't have a fit and a half.

A haddock, a haddock, a black-spotted haddock,
A black spot on the black back of a black-spotted
haddock.

Was that your ewer of yore?

Shelters shield shivering sheep.

The rat ran by the river with a lump of raw liver.

Should a shad, shelling shrimps for a shark,
Cease to shuck the shamed shrimps who remark,
"Serve us not without dressing!
"It is really distressing,"
Or should he shuck shrimps in the dark?

Shadows shade the sheltered shallows.

Six Scotch soldiers shooting snipe.

Shy Sheila sat shivering in her slim shiny shot-silk
smock.

I see a ship in sight of the shore.

Black bug's blood.

This is the catastrophic hypothesis of the suppositious
apothecary.

One old owl occupies an old oak.

A tree toad loved a she toad
That lived up in a tree.
He was a two-toed tree toad,
While a three-toed toad was she.
The he-toad tree toad tried to gain
The she toad's friendly nod,
For the two-toed tree toad loved the ground
That the three-toed tree toad trod.
The two-toed tree toad tried in vain
But couldn't please her whim,
For from her tree toad bower
With her she-toad power
The three-toed tree toad vetoed him.

Jean, Joan, George, and Gerald judged generally.

A jester from Leicester went to see Esther, but as Esther
was taking her siesta, the jester from Leicester didn't see
Esther.

The tiresome wireless man's fireless,
Whilst the fireless wireless man's tireless.

You can have—
Fried fresh fish,
Fish fried fresh,
Fresh fried fish,
Fresh fish fried,
Or fish fresh fried.

Ten tongue-tied tailors twisted tinted thistles with their
teeth. If ten tongue-tied tailors twisted tinted thistles with
their teeth, who tinted the tinted thistles that the ten
tongue-tied tailors twisted?

A fine field of wheat,
A field of fine wheat.

Let us go together to gather lettuce
Whether the weather will let us or no.

The skunk sat on the stump and thunk the stump stunk.
But the stump thunk the skunk stunk.

Bill had a billboard.
Bill also had a board bill
Which bored Bill
Until Bill sold his billboard
And paid his board bill.
Then the board bill
No longer bored Bill,
But though he had no board bill,
Neither did he have his billboard!

Twisty twining twirling tendrils
Tethering together tightly
Ten tall trees.

Through the thicket and bush the thirty thirsty Thracians
thrust.

Students study stencilling steadily.

Snow slipping slowly sliding sideways.

Now, a sleeping car's known as a sleeper,
And sleepers for sleepers they keep,
And sleepers run under the sleepers
In which those sleepy sleepers all sleep.
If a top was to sleep in a sleeper
And the sleeper beneath him went pop,
It's logical cert that the top would get hurt,
For there's no sleeper that sleeps like a top.

A skunk jumped over a stump in a skunk hole.

Shallow shores show some sign of sunshine.

I saw Esau kissing Kate.
Fact is, we all three saw.
I saw Esau, he saw me,
And she saw I saw Esau.

Nestlings nestle nightly in their nests.

Lots of little London lamplighters,
Light London's lot of little lamps.

Do drop in at Dewdrop Inn.

Once upon a barren moor
There dwelt a bear, also a boar.
The bear could not bear the boar,
The boar thought the bear a bore.
At last the bear could bear no more
That boar that bored him on the moor.
And so one morn he bored the boar—
That boar will bore the bear no more.

A big blue bug bit a big black bear,
Made a big black bear bleed blood.

As round the rough and rugged rock the ragged
rascal ran.

Down the slippery slide they slid
Sitting slightly sideways;
Slipping swiftly see them skid
On holidays and Fridays.

A pale pink proud peacock pompously preened its pretty
plumage.

Dr. Fowler Sneed Freeman, the daring, darling dentist
from Dorset, would fairly flounder without a fullness of
floss.

A truly rural frugal ruler's mural.

A shooting suit that's suitable for shooting,
Should be made of a suiting that is suitable;
If not made of suiting that is suitable,
Then that shooting suit's not suitable for shooting.

Where wizened wranglers wield weighty windows,
winsome wrinkles weirdly wrangle whitened windows.

The wild wolf roams the wintry wastes.

Swan, swim over the sea.
Swim, swim, swim!
Swan, swim back again.
Well swum, swan!

The minx mixed a medicinal mixture.

The poor dog's paw poured water from every pore.

Penelope Pringle printed press photographs.

My dame hath a lame tame crane.
My dame hath a crane that is lame.
Pray, gentle Jane, let my dame's tame crane
Feed and come home again.

The sixth sheik's sixth sheep's sick.

Oswald Whittle's whistle out-whistles all other
whistlers' whistles in Oswaldtwistle.

I bought the blazer braid I bought to bind the blazer blue.
The braid I bought was not too bright to bind the blazer
blue.

A shy little she said, "Shoo!"
To a fly and a flea in a flue.

"Are you copper bottoming 'em, my man?"
"No, I'm alumining 'em, Mum!"

A big beadle placed a body in a big black bag.

Pete's pa, Pete, poked to the pea patch to pick a peck of peas for the poor pink pig in the pinehole pig pen.

Six twin-screw cruisers.

Bill Badger brought the bear a bit of boiled bacon in a brown bag.

Seventy shuddering sailors standing silent as short, sharp, shattering shocks shake their splendid ship.

Oporto, a port in Portugal, exports port.

The beet that beat the beet that beat the other beet is now beaten by the beet that beats all the beets, whether the original beet that beat the beet or the beet that beat the beet that beat the other beet.

Bandy-legg'd Borachio Mustachio Whiskerifusticus, the Bald and Brave Bombandino of Bagdad, helped Abomilique Bluebeard Bashaw of Babelmandel to beat down the abominable bumblebee at Balsora.

Brenda Blenkin braised a box of British bloaters,
A box of British bloaters Brenda Blenkin braised;
If Brenda Blenkin braised a box of British bloaters,
Where's the box of British bloaters Brenda Blenkin braised?

Tuesday is stew day.
Stew day is Tuesday.

Gig-whip.

Bill Wood said he would carry the wood through the wood and if Wood said he would, Wood would.

Peter Payntor the painter prefers painting pink pigs to picking pretty purple pansies.

For fine fresh fish phone Phil.

Pure food for four pure mules.

The woman wound wool well while the wild wind whistled.

The mister whose sister has a blister hissed incessantly with hysterical bluster.

Langley left Lofton in Boston often.

The town's clown frowns when the clown town's down.

The thesaurus to Lazarus was useless when used to excessive abuses.

The Hebrew blew the bugle lugubriously.

If a sleeper, in a sleeper sleeps, does not the sleeper not in the sleeper on the sleeper sleep?

For a shilling Sherri sold Thad's thimble.

Charlie shall share shares Sally sold short.

Red leather, yellow leather,
Red leather, yellow leather.

Shred and shrew the shroud and shrub shrivel and shrink the shrike.

I went into my garden to slay snails.
I saw my little slave slaying snails.
I said, "Hello, my little slave, are you slaying snails?
If you slay snails, slay small snails."

Mother Smucker would allow no one to tuck her,
Except brother Tucker who was a Mother Smucker
tucker.

"Do daring deeds do damage," demanded Doctor
Doolittle.

An artist went to sea to see what he could see at sea to
draw, but all the artist saw at sea is what we always see
at sea—see?

Your Bob owes our Bob a bob, and if your Bob doesn't
give our Bob that bob your Bob owes our Bob, our Bob
will give your Bob a bob on the nob.

Pretty Polly Perkin polished pastel plates and plaster
plaques.

Mrs. Biggar had a baby. Which was the bigger?
The baby we know was a little Biggar, but what of Mr.
Biggar who was father Biggar? However, Mr. Biggar
died. Was the baby then bigger than Mrs. Biggar? No,
the baby was no bigger. Why? Because the baby had
become fatherless.

Do breath tests test the breath?
Yes, that's the best of a breath test.
So the best breath stands the breath test best.

Greek grapes.

A big blue bucket of blue blueberries.

Double bubble gum bubbles double.

A big blue badly bleeding blister.

A monk's monkey mounted a monastery wall and munched melon and macaroni.

Frances Fowler's father fried five floundering flounders for Frances Fowler's father's father.

Mr. McComb missed his missus but didn't miss her listlessness.

A bloke's back brake block broke.

Manassas is fast with lasses but slow as molasses in classes so Manassas never passes.

A pale pink proud peacock pompously preened its pretty plumage.

Bunty's brother bought a British brush to brush Bunty's brown brogues.

Many million Mini-Minors merrily milling 'round Manchester.

I never smelled a smelt that smelled as bad as that smelt smelled.

Mr. Poynter owned a pretty pointer who pointed only pheasants and that was Poynter's plight.
For pheasants present when Poynter's pointer pointed pheasants flitted forth in a fit of flight.

"Brighton Belle" banging British bones.

May Messant may,
But Maisie May mustn't.

Put the cut pumpkin in a pipkin.

Truly rural, purely plural, truly rurally, purely plurally.

Lotty licks lollies lolling in the lobby.

Brandon often expanded offhanded on landings where landed dandies pranced grandly.

"The bun is better buttered," Billy muttered.

The bleak breeze blights the bright bloom blossom.

A nightingale knew no night was nicer than a nice night to sing his nocturnals.

A tidy tiger tied a tie tighter to tidy her tiny tail.

Sly Sam sips Sally's soup.

Ned's keg bled red, red bled Ned's keg.

A lump of red leather, a red leather lump.

I want a dozen double damask dinner napkins.

Lovely lilacs line Lee's lonely lane.

Reading bells ring rapidly and reeds rustle 'round rivers.

Nine nimble noblemen nibble nuts.

Sylvia succinctly stated cerebral statements satisfying sanctimonious scoffers.

Six sportsmen shooting snipe.

Heather was hoping to hop to Tahiti
To hack a hibiscus to hang on her hat.
Now Heather has hundreds of hats on her hat rack,
So how can a hop to Tahiti help that?

Oh, Horace! Isn't it horrible when you're hot and in a hurry and you've got to hold your hat in your hand.

Bees horde heaps of honey in hives.

Shy Susie Shipton sewed seams on Sammy's Sunday shirt.

Children chuckle cheerily.

Richard gave Robin a rap in the ribs for roasting a rabbit so rare.

Silas shingles singularly Sunday's but is shunned for singular Sabbath shingling.

If a shipshape ship shop stocks six shipshape ships, how many shipshape shop-soiled ships would six shipshape ship shops stock?

Futile Philip forced Frank to fence.

Fancy Nancy didn't fancy work, but fancy Nancy's fancy auntie did fancy fancy Nancy doing fancy work.

Fetch fifty-five foils!

Six Swiss ships swiftly shift.

The sunshade sheltered Sarah from the sunshine.

Barbara burned the brown bread badly.

The Swiss witch which bewitched this switch wished the switch bewitched.

She sells sea shells, sherry, and sandals on the seashore.

Mr. Custer cloistered mustard, hundreds in his
cupboard.
Mrs. Custer mustered diamonds that out lustered Mr.
Custer's mustard.

She stops at the shops where I shop,
And if she shops at the shops where I shop
I won't stop at the shop where she shops.

Lemon liniment.

The crisp crust crackles crunchily.

Hull has huge houses and high holidays.

With a shovel Sarah slowly shifted sifted cinders.

The chilly sited click steel slitter sitting slitting satellite's
charted sits.

Vigorous Vests voiced voluble verse vociferously.

Once a feller
Met a feller
In a field of beans,
Said the feller
To a feller
Can a feller
Tell a feller
What a feller means?

Famous friezes figured fabulously.

Good blood, bad blood.

Oscar's order caused disorder on the badlands border.

The fat-thighed freak fries thick fish.

The rain ceaseth and sufficeth us.

Softly, silently, the scythe
Slithered through the thick sweet sward;
Seething, sweating, sad serfs writhe,
Slicing swaths so straight and broad.

One old ox opening oysters.

I'm a critical cricket critic.

Cross-eyed Clara's
Crazy over crosswords,
She's got competitions on the brain—
When she's working—everybody's weary
She's wrapped up in her dictionary—
Ma's cross, Pa's cross,
King's Cross, Charing Cross,
Everybody's got cross ways
And it's quite imposs—
To avoid getting cross
With cross-eyed Clara and her crossword craze.

A cup of creamy custard
Cook cooked for Cuthbert.

Theophilus Thistledown,
The successful thistle sifter,
In sifting a sieve of unsifted thistles,
Thrust three thousand thistles
Through the thick of his thumb.
If then, Theophilus Thistledown,
The successful thistle sifter,
Thrust three thousand thistles
Through the thick of his thumb,
See that thou,
In sifting a sieve of thistles,
Do not get the unsifted thistles
Stuck in thy thumb.

English usage, what's the use,
When persimmon follows puce.

Typical tropical trivial trite trash.

The saucy slippery scoundrel scampered scurrying by.

Twenty tinkers took two hundred tin tacks to Toy Town.
If twenty tinkers took two hundred tin tacks to Toy
Town, how many tin tacks did each of the twenty tinkers
going to Toy Town take?

Stories stop steady study.

Though a kiss be amiss
She who misses the kisses,
A Miss without kisses,
May miss being Mrs.

Snerdly slyly snickered wryly.

A plain plywood police van,
Privately packed with protesting passengers,
Plies periodically to Plymouth prison.

Bunty's brother brought a British brush to brush
Bunty's brown brogues.

British brown bells boosting "Back Britain" broaches.

Nina needs nine knitting needles to knit naughty Nita's
knickers nicely.

Sue said she should show the shrewd shrew the same
shoe she threw through.

When his hat hit Horace, Horace hollered.

A tall eastern girl named Short long loved a big Mr. Little. But Little, thinking little of Short, loved a little lass named Long. To belittle Long, Short announced she would marry Little before long. This caused Little to shortly marry Long. To make a long story short, did tall Short love big Little less because Little loved little Long more?

Rich Rajahs ride reindeers with red rope reins round their regal necks.

Now nice nurses need necklaces.

Sixty-six slick Salvationists.

Timothy Taylor twiddled tightly twisted twine ten times to test it.

Beth Smith.

Sam sat with his jaw set as he sat watching a set sitting on a wet cement settee,
"I've never seen a set sit on wet cement, and they will keep sitting because they will soon be set," said he.

Simon Short, Smithfield's sole surviving shoemaker.

A cricket critic cricked his neck at a critical cricket match.

I often sit and think and fish and sit and fish and think and sit and fish—and think—and wish that I could get a drink.

Oh! that I was where I would be,
Then would I be where I am not;
But where I am I must be,
And where I would be, I cannot.

They thanked them thoroughly.

I'm a fig plucker,
I'm a fig plucker's son,
I pluck figs till the fig pluckers come.

A selfish shellfish smelt a stale fish.
If the stale fish was smelt
Then the selfish shellfish smelt a smelt.

Say this sharply, say this sweetly,
Say this shortly, say this softly,
Say this sixteen times in succession.

Hiram wrote a hymn for him to hum, but his hymn he
couldn't hum so he had his hymn hummed by other
than he.

Sheila's Shetland pony shied.
Shooting Sheila on the shore.
Shaking Sheila, stupefied,
Struggled homeward stiff and sore.

Three thumping tigers tickling trout.

How many cuckoos could a good Cook cook if a good
Cook could cook cuckoos?
If a good Cook could cook cuckoos so fine
And a good Cook could cook cuckoos all the time,
How many cuckoos could a good Cook cook
If a good Cook could cook cuckoos?

A Glasgow glazier's gloriously gleaming green glass
gas-globes.

Phil Fine filched fine pine.

Cleans terminal screens without streaking.

Premoistened pads of isopropyl properties properly
penetrate.

Shrewd Simon Short sewed shoes. Seventeen summers saw Simon's small, shabby shop still standing, saw Simon's selfsame squeaking sign still swinging swiftly, specifying:

SIMON SHORT
Smithfield's Sole Surviving
SHOEMAKER
Shoes Soled—Sewed Superfinely

Simon's spouse, Sally Short, sewed sheets, stitched shirts, stuffed sofas.

Simon's stout sturdy sons—Stephen, Samuel, Saul, Silas—sold sundries. Stephen sold silks, satins, shawls. Samuel sold saddles, stirrups. Saul sold silver spoons, specialties. Silas sold Sally Short's stuffed sofas.

Simon's second son, Samuel, saw Sophia Sophronia Spriggs somewhere. Sweet, sensible, smart Sophia Sophronia Spriggs. Sam soon showed strange symptoms. Surprisingly, Sam sighed sorrowfully, sang several serenades slyly, sought Sophia Spriggs' society, seldom stood selling saddles.

Simon stormed, scowled severely, said, "Sam seems so silly singing such senseless songs."

"Softly," said sweet Sally. "Sam's smitten. Sam's spied some sweetheart."

"Smitten!" snarled Simon. "Scatterbrained simpleton! Sentimental schoolboy!"

Sally sighed sadly. Summoning Sam, she spoke sympathizingly. "Sam," said she, "Sire* seems singularly snappish. So, Sonny, stop strolling streets so soberly, stop singing sly serenades. Sell saddles sensibly, Sam. See Sophia Sophronia Spriggs speedily."

* Father

"So soon?" said Sam, startled.

"Son soon, surely," said Sally, smilingly, "specially since Sire shows such spirit."

So Sam, somewhat scared, sauntered slowly storeward, shaking stupendously. "Sophia Sophronia Spriggs . . . Sam's Short spouse . . . sounds splendid," said Sam softly.

Sam soon spied Sophia starching shirts, singing softly. Seeing Sam, she stopped, saluting Sam smilingly.

Sam stuttered shockingly. "Sp-sp-splendid s-s-summer s-s-season, So-So-Sophia."

"Somewhat sultry," suggested Sophia.

"S-s-sartin,"** said Sam.

"Still selling saddles, Sam?" said Sophia.

"S-s-sartin," said Sam.

Silence, seventeen seconds.

"Sire shot sixteen snipe Saturday, Sam," said Sophia.

Silence, seventy-seven seconds.

"See sister Sue's sunflowers," said Sophia socially, stopping such stiff silence.

Such sprightly sauciness stimulated Sam strangely. So, swiftly speaking, Sam said, "Sue's sunflowers seem saying, 'Sophia Sophronia Spriggs, Samuel Shorts stroll serenely, seek some sparkling streams, sing some sweet, soul-stirring strain . . .'"

Sophia snickered, so Sam stopped. She stood silently several seconds.

Said Sam, "Stop smiling, Sophia. Sam's seeking some sweet spouse!"

She still stood silently.

"Speak, Sophia, speak! Such silence speculates sorrow."

"Seek Sire Spriggs, Sam," said Sophia.

Sam sought Sire Spriggs.

Sire Spriggs said, "Sartin."

* Certainly

Will real wheels really wheel?

As I was going by Mrs. King's yard,
I saw a man sawing,
And of all the sawers I ever saw,
I never saw a saw saw like that saw sawed.

Now a twister of a twist, he twisted some twist,
And the twist that he twisted was a twelve twisted twist,
But if one single twist of that twelve twisted twist was to
come untwisted,
I would spoil all the twist that the twister
Of the twelve twisted twist had twisted.

The Jew, Hugh, knew blue news, but the few who
knew Hugh knew the blue news was Hugh's views and
refused to be blued by the blue news Jew Hugh knew.

The dustman daily does his duty to dislodge the dirty
dust deposited in disgusting dusty dustbins.

The gnu grew to think Lou knew,
But the gnu learned Lou knew nothing;
So the gnu eschewed Lou and Lou scorned the gnu
For the gnu knew less than Lou knew.

Knott was not in;
Knott was out
Knotting knots in netting;
Knott was out
But lots of knots
Were in Knott's notty netting.

The tailor's cutter cluttered the table with Scotch Cheviot
cuttings.

The Swiss miss gave the twist a Swiss twist,
Twisting Swissly this way and thusly.

Two boot blacks, a white boot black and a black boot black, stood together doing nothing.

The white boot black proposed that he should black the boots of the black boot black.

The black boot black was perfectly willing to have his boots blacked by the white boot black.

So the white boot black began to black the boots of the black boot black.

But when the white boot black had blacked one boot of the black boot black, he decided not to black the other boot of the black boot black, until the black boot black had blacked both boots of the white boot black.

However, the black boot black refused point blank to black the boots of the white boot black, and said he didn't care whether the white boot black blacked the other boot black or not.

He considered that one boot blacked was enough for a black boot black to black, and that a black boot black with one boot blacked was better than a white boot black with no boots blacked.

Then the white boot black called the black boot black a black blackguard.

Of course, when the white boot black began blacking the character of the black boot black, the black boot black began blacking the face of the white boot black all black with the blacking on the boots the white boot black had blacked, and the white boot black blacked the black boot black back.

When the society of Black and White Boot Blackers considered the matter, they characterized the conduct of both boot blacks as the blackest affair that had ever blackened the pages of boot black history.

A purely rural duel truly plural is better than a purely plural duel truly rural.

While trying to whistle
Christopher Twistle
twisted his tongue.

A Teflon zeppelin.

A clipper ship shipped several clipped sheep.
Were these clipped sheep the clipper ship's sheep?
Or just clipped sheep shipped on a clipper ship?

We had a knocker-up, and our knocker-up had a
knocker-up, and our knocker-up's knocker-up didn't
knock our knocker-up up, so our knocker-up didn't
knock us up.

If Timothy Theophylliss Thicklewade Thackham thrust
his two thick thumbs through three hundred and thirty-
three thousand three hundred and thirty-three thick and
thin thistles, where are the three hundred and thirty-three
thousand three hundred and thirty-three thick and thin
thistles that Timothy Theophylliss Thicklewade
Thackham thrust his two thick thumbs through?

Then the thankless theologian thawed thoroughly.

The school coal in the school coal scuttle was scattered
by a cool scholar.

Old Tommy Taylor, tailor, and retailer,
Doth retail old army coats and also coats of mail;
With coats of paint, he paints his coat of arms above
    his door.
His motto is: I sew the tears, that all may rip the more.

This is a zither.

Three tree twigs.

Give George green gloves and gleaming goulashes.

Six slim saplings.

Soot is smut that's up a flue.

Swamps thick six,
Six thick swamps.

The Archbishop's cat crept craftily into Canterbury
Cathedral crypt causing cataclysmal chaos in clerical
circles by keeping cunningly concealed.

Six thin thistle sticks.

If Thornwick and Thornbag Thistledown Thostledown,
pushed their thick thumbs through thick and thin thistles,
where are the thick and thin thistles that Thornwick and
Thornbag Thistledown, pushed their thick thumbs
through?

Really rural.

Forty fat farmers found a field of fine fresh fodder.
Now, if forty fat farmers found a field of fine fresh
fodder, where is the field of fine fresh fodder those forty
farmers found?

You snuff shop snuff.
I sniff shop snuff.

This thistle seems like that thistle.

I need not your needles
They're needless to me,
For needing needles
Is needless you see.
But did my neat trousers
But need to be kneed,
I then should have need
Of your needles indeed.

Silly Sammy Stokes split some sticky syrup on the
stove.

This is what an indignant man is said to have said to his friend who said he said "I say" to everything his friend said: "I say, so-and-so, they say you say I say 'I say' to everything you say. Even if it is so, so-and-so, and I do say 'I say' to everything you say, you shouldn't say I say 'I say' to everything you say.

The horses' hard hoofs hit the hard high road.

His shirt soon shrank in the suds.

A maid in Grantham, Mum,
Once played the National Anthem, Mum,
And broke a chrysanthemum, Mum.

Is it better to ride in a car and think it is better to ride in a car than it is to walk and think it is better to ride in a car than it is to walk?

Once I heard mother utter,
"Daughter, go and shut the shutter."
"Shutter's shut," the daughter uttered,
"For I can't shut it any shutter."

It ain't the hunting on the hills that hurts the horse's hoofs, it's the hammer, hammer, hammer, on the hard high road.

The shepherd shares the Shetland shawl.

Our Joe wants to know if your Joe will lend our Joe your banjo. If your Joe won't lend our Joe your Joe's banjo, our Joe won't lend your Joe's banjo when our Joe has a banjo.

The fish sauce shop's sure to sell sauce for my fish.

Preshrunk shirts.

She saw thirty-four swift sloops swing shorewards,
before she saw the forty-three spaceships soar.

Five French friars fanning a fainted flea.

Three Scotch thistles in the thicket.

The Leith police dismisseth us.

Does this shop stock short socks with spots?

Ten thatchers went to thatch ten tiny thatched cottages,
taking ten tight bundles of thatching straw with them to
thatch with.

A thatcher was thatching a thatch.
"Good morning, thatcher,
The next time you thatch a thatch,
Thatch a thick thatch, thatcher."

The Duke dragged the dizzy Dane deep down into the
damp dark dungeon.

Sister Susy sneezes slightly,
Slicing succulent shallots.

A shifty snake selling snake skin slippers.

Wishy-washy Wilfred wished to win a wager.

A peck of pickled pepper Peter Piper picked;
If Peter Piper picked a peck of pickled pepper,
Where's the peck of pickled pepper Peter Piper picked?

Simpson sweated shifting sifted saffron into thick sacks.

Blood red bed bugs.

Sarah saw a sash shop full of showy, shiny sashes.

Racing this way and that with lips pursed Pushkin placed ottomans oddly askew knowing many men tired from trudging fens found solace sharing sitting space throughout the inn.

Big brown bumblebees were buried beside the bulbs in Bobby Brook's bulb bowls, baskets, and boxes.

Betty Blue blows big black bubbles.

"Mortals may not match my magic," muttered the magician menacingly.

A single solid silver sifter sifts sifted sugar.

Tommy Tickle tickled his teacher. Where did Tommy Tickle's teacher tickle Tommy?

A kiss is the anatomical juxtaposition of two orbicularis oris muscles in a state of contraction.

Cheerful children chant charming tunes.

She saw the shiny soap suds sailing down the shallow sink.

How high His Highness holds his haughty head.

A bloke's back brake block broke.

I wonder whither the weather will waft the wherry wherein the weather is, and whether the whether and wherry will weather the weather?

Cheap ship trips.

The dude dropped in at the Dewdrop Inn.

The slippery shoat slithered shedward.

Shelly served chilly chili to silly Sally.
Serving chilly chili to silly Sally Shelly said,
"Stir it soundly, silly, chili chilly will become more
chilly surely if you stir chilly chili willy-nilly."

Mother made Mary, Minnie, and Molly march many
times round the room to martial music.

Let little Nellie run a little

A ship saileth south soon.

Mrs. Pipple Popple popped a pebble in poor Polly
Pepper's eye.

Is that the Lord Mayor's mare?

Little Willie's wooden whistle wouldn't whistle.

Unique New York.

Strange strategic statistics.

Georgia's gorge is gorgeous.

Have you prepared the gooseberries, Mary?"
I'm just topping and bottoming 'em, Mum."

He bade him eat his own hot ham so his own hot ham
he ate.

The chased treasure chest's thrice chipped.

Phil's pills kill chills—
Chills Phil's pills kill.

Dempster's hamster, Mister Dunston, doffed his derby
to a charming gerbil evoking gerbil garble.

She chews cream cheese and fresh cress sandwiches.

"Help! Help!" harassedly howled the hunted Huguenot.

Shoppers flocking shopping—
Shocking shoppers shopping.

Cheryl's cheap chip shop sells cheap chips.

There was an old lady called Carr;
Who took the three-three for Forfar;
She said, "I believe
It's sure to leave
Before the four-four for Forfar."

One violet winkle veering west via Worthing went
wading round Ventnor.

Three thrushes thrilled them.

She is a thistle sifter, and she has a sieve of sifted
thistles, and a sieve of unsifted thistles, and the sieve of
unsifted thistles she sieves into the sieve of sifted
thistles, because she is s thistle sifter.

"I can think of thin things, six thin things, can you?"
"Yes, I can think of six thin things, and of six thick
things too."

Cliff Cross crossed the criss-cross crossing.
The criss-cross crossing Cliff Cross crossed.
When Cliff Cross crossed the criss-cross crossing,
Where's the criss-cross crossing Cliff Cross crossed?

Thin-skinned Slim, thinking Theda's statements
scurrilous, scolded scathingly.

Strikes strangle struggle squandering scheduled
synthesis.

A canner, exceedingly canny,
One day remarked to his granny—
"A canner can can
Anything he can,
But a canner can't can a can, can he?"

Ten penny tinkers tinkering tenpenny tinder tins.

The troops tread the toilsome trail.

The apples fermented inside the lamented and made cider
inside her inside.

The twenty-to-two train to Tooting tooted tunefully as it
tore through the tunnel.

The royal lady received the roses regally at the recent
reception.

A glowing gleam glowing green.

Gaily gathered the gleaners the glossy golden grain,
And garnered it gladly
In Granny's great granary
In Godfrey's green grassy glen.

Look at the pug tugging the rug.

The Ku-Klux-Klan can't find a cold cure.

I'd far rather lather father,
Than father lather me,
Because when father lathers,
He lathers rather free.

cute

There are thirty thousand feathers on that there thrush's
throat.

Fancy Fanny Franks feeling funny about Fred Ferraby's fishing flies for Fred Ferraby fishes with flies to catch frisky fishes.

Chimes challenged the changing year.

Simon Squirrel sold Swiss roll and shiny salt shrimps swatched in Shetland pink shawls.

The shuddering soldier shrugs his shoulders.

Hams hung up,
Hung up hams.

Out of his hole to steal he stole,
His bag of chink and chunk,
And many a wicked smile he smole,
And many a wink he wunk.

Has Helen heard how Hilda hurried home?

She sells shells, snowshoes, and sweet sherry.

Some say sweet-scented shaving soap soothes sore skins.

Collectible classics cause considerable consternation among auto aficionados.

He knew when he blew at a Hebrew he blew at that Hebrews never blew back.

Short shrift.

Seven shivering sailors swam steadily shoreward;
Seventh sailor shouted, "Swim swiftly—sighted shark!"

The first fast master passed faster than the last fast pastor.

Stop chop shops selling chopped shop chops.

Jingling George jingled gherkins in a jar.

Chief Sheik, sheep section.

Three fluffy feathers fell from Phoebe's fan.

Fresh fried flesh of fowl.

Questing Quidnunc quizzed a queerish question.
Did Questing Quidnunc quiz a queerish question?
If Questing Quidnunc quizzed a queerish question,
What's the queerish question Questing Quidnunc
quizzed?

The wild wind whipped Whit from the wharf.

Which wristwatches are Swiss wristwatches?

Tom threw Tim three thumbtacks.

A black-backed bath brush.

Silver thimbles.

The two twenty-two tore through town.

'Lisbeth lips lengthy lessons.

He generally reads regularly in a government library
particularly rich in Coptic manuscripts except during the
month of February.

Thirty thousand Thracians threatened Thessaly.

A queer quick questioning quiz.

Literally literary literature.

On two thousand acres too tangled for tilling,
Where thousands of thorn trees grew thrifty
  and thrilling,
Theophilus Twistle, less thrifty than some,
Thrust three thousand thistles through the thick
  of his thumb.

Blame the big bleak black book!

Round and round the rugged rock the ragged rascal ran.

Three sick thrushes sang thirty-six thrilling songs.

Master said that that that is the right that in that particular
place.

I thought I thought a thought. But the thought I thought I
thought wasn't the thought I thought I thought. If the
thought I thought I thought had been the thought I
thought, I wouldn't have thought so much.

Two thirsty thatchers thoughtfully thatched a thrush's
nest. Such a thankless task.

The threaded beads thrilled them.

I went into the garden
Where I saw five brave maids
Sitting on five broad beds
Braiding broad braids.
I said to these five maids
Sitting on five broad beds
Braiding broad braids,
"Braid broad braids, brave maids."

Through six thick swamps stumbled Sammy.

Thus the thug threatened the thoroughly thoughtful
theologist.

Babbling Bert blamed Bess.

Miss Ruth's red roof thatch.

Shy Sheila shakes soft shimmering silks.

The thatched roof is thick.

Which is the witch that wished the wicked wish?

Three thrice-freed thieves.

Sir Cecil Thistlethwaite, the celebrated theological statistician.

Wheedling, weeping Winne wails wildly.

Five fashionable females flying to France for fresh fashions.

Is there a pleasant peasant present?

Francis fries fish fillets for Frederick.
Frederick fillets fish for Francis' fried fritters.

Tim, the thin twin tinsmith.

Shoes and socks shock Susie.

Frisky Freddy feeds on fresh fried fish.

"Sheath thy sword," the surly sheriff said,
"Or surely shall a churlish serf soon shatter thee."

Shipshape suit shops ship shapely suits.

Wise wives whistle while weaving worsted waistcoats.

The sun shines on shop signs.

Six silly sisters sell silk to six sickly seniors.

Three fiddling pigs sat in a pit and fiddled;
Fiddle, piggy, fiddle, piggy, fiddle, piggy.

Charlie chooses cheese and cherries.

Shall Sarah Silling share her silver shilling?
Sarah Silling shall share her shining shilling.

The winkle ship sank and the shrimp ship swam.

Bonnie bliss blows big beautiful bubbles.

My wife gave Mr. Snipe's wife's knife a swipe.

Six short soldiers sang a short song while scrubbing six
short shirts sister Susie sewed.

Till Tom taught tact to Tim,
Tim talked tosh to tots.

I never felt felt that felt like that felt felt.

Ten tiny toddling tots trying to train their tongues to trill.

Sam Slick sawed six slimy, slippery side saplings.

Saucy Sally saw silly Sam sowing sunflower seeds.
If silly Sam saw saucy Sally seeing him sow sunflower
seeds, should Sam sob?

Miss MacIntyre's tiresome tire of her tricycle twisted.

Tom threw three thumbtacks.

We surely shall see the sun shine soon.

Yellow Yo-yos.

Don't run along the wrong lane.

Lucy lingered, looking longingly for her lost lapdog.

'Round and 'round the rugged rock the ragged rascal
runs his truly rural race.

Lucie listened to the lilt of the lark.

Sooty Sukey
Shook some soot
From Sister Susie's
Sooty shoes.

The twister of twists once twisted a twist,
And the twist he was twisting was a three-twisted twist,
And untwisting this twist one became untwisted,
And untwisted the twist that the twister was twisting.

A woman in a plaid shawl shovelled soft snow slowly.

William Whiteley's washhouse windows want well
washing with warm water.

Michael and Moses have very keen noses
And very fine hoses for watering roses.

Rubber baby buggy bumpers.

I go by a Blue Goose bus.

A queer quick questioning quiz.

Beautiful babbling brooks bubble between blossoming
banks.

Some shun sunshine.
Bisquick—kiss quick!

The brisk brave brigadiers brandished broad bright blades, blunderbusses, and bludgeons.

Am I and Amy aiming anaemic anemones on my many enemies?

Freckled-faced Florence.

The three-three leaves Leith before the four-four for Forfar.

Chin-chin Chang, chop! chop! chop!

Joan joyously joined jaunty John in jingling jigs.

Suppose Sally shredded suet so swiftly that she was sooner done than she expected, how slowly would Sally have to shred suet to be done as soon as she expected she would?

He ran from the Indies to the Andes in his undies.

Thin sticks, thick bricks.

"Has Hugh heavily harassed him?"

Sheila is selling shelled shrimps.

Susan Schumann shot a solitary chamois and received a short sharp salutary shock for such shameless slaughter.

Please sell me some short silk socks and some shimmering satin sashes.

Cross crossings cautiously!

Seventy shuddering sailors stood silent as short sharp shattering shocks shook the splendid ship.

Three free thugs set three thugs free.

Six thick thistle sticks.

The conundrum constructed by the communist was catastrophical.

Quick quiet quills quote Quinney's quarrel.

Kate's tasty hasty cakes.

The crime completed, the coward crawled cautiously coastward.

Mr. Knox
Keeps his socks
In a pale pink chocolate box—
Orange socks
With spots and clocks.

Mr. See owned a saw
And Mr. Soar owned a seesaw.
Now See's saw sawed Soar's seesaw
Before Soar saw See
Which made Soar sore.
Had Soar seen See's saw
Before See sawed Soar's seesaw,
See's saw would not have sawed Soar's seesaw.
So See's saw sawed Soar's seesaw.
But it was a shame to see Soar so sore
Just because See's saw sawed Soar's seesaw.

Naughty Nettie's knitting knotted nighties for the Navy.

You slipped. I saw you slip on that slip of slide on which you slipped.

A laurel-crowned clown.

Polly Cox's ox ate eight hollyhocks. Now the
eight-hollyhocks-eating-ox lies in a blue-black box.

The cringing coon cowered in the corner.

I buy my clothes from Theophilus Thistlethwaite the
clothier at thirty-three Twelfth Street.

Five flashy flappers,
Flitting forth fleetly,
Found four flighty flappers,
Flirting flippantly.

Flee from fog to fight flu fast.

The graves gamesman groused when the greyhound
growled.

She stood on the balcony inexplicably mimicking him
hiccuping and welcoming him in.

Gay gallants gambolling on the green grass.

A crazy crooked critic.

Ten tons of pink tinted toilet tissues to Timothy Tims of
Tooting.

Thirty-six teasle tweezer trees.

Stalk stags silently.

Seven Severn salmon swallowing shrimps.

Nine nimble noblemen nibbling nasty knobby nuts.

I slit the sheet and the sheet slit me.
Slitten was the sheet that was slit by me.

Choose stew Tuesday,
Tuesday is stew day.

A dozen dozen double damask dinner napkins.

The wire wound around a reel.

Our black bull bled black blood on our blackthorn
flower.

Many an anemone sees an enemy anemone.

Black dog danced on the barn floor barefooted.

A bearded peer on the pier appeared to peer in the beer
glass.

And ere her ear had heard her heart had heard.

Shiver and slither shovelling slushy squelchy snow.

Virile Victor vanquished vain vendors.

Tom bought some fine prime pink popcorns from the
prime pink popcorn shop.

Greengages grow in greengage trees.

Twelve tall tulips turning to the sun.

Swan swam over the sea—well swum swan.

Nine nimble noblemen nibbling nettles.

Dancing dangerously down the dale dainty Dinah dashed
dizzily past Dorothy.

Stanley stood sturdy and strong.

The desperado designed the desperate plot to dupe the dreadful dramatist.

Conrad came careening round the corner, completing his crazy career by crashing into the crypt.

Three grey-green greedy geese,
Feeding on a weedy piece.
The piece was weedy,
And the geese were greedy,
Three grey-green greedy geese.

Frightened fluffy fowls flying foolishly through the farmyard.

She mixed gruel in a bowl and set it out for fowl;
Finding the gruel foul the fowl flew south.

Alice McAlister sliced slaw into salad.

Hardy Harry Harnick heaved heavily with heartfelt honesty having honored Sam's sister Charlotte.

The schlemiel slopped several servings before stopping serving slopped servings.

They tried to temp the tattered tramps to take the toothsome tarts.

Pretty Polly pressed porous poultices politely to putty, Patricia practicing polite patience as the porous poultices to pouty Patricia were pressed.

Twas brillig, and the slithy toves
  Did gyre and gimble in the wabe;
All misty were the borogoves,
  And the nome raths outgrabe.

A ship saileth south soon.